Origins

The Deep

Margaret Su ■ Anthony Hope-Smith

OXFORD
UNIVERSITY PRESS

2

Chapter 1 - Good morning!

A female voice broke the morning silence. "Please wake up." The lights in the room flicked on. In the soft glow, two boys were visible, fast asleep in their beds. George and Calvin continued to snore. For a few minutes, it was the only sound in the room. Then the female voice repeated, "Please wake up."

Five minutes later, George and Calvin's beds gently tipped them face-down onto the floor. Two T-shirts and two pairs of trousers shot out of the wall and landed near their feet. Silently their beds slid into the walls.

Sleepily, George picked up a T-shirt. It read: "I ♥ hermit crabs." There was a picture of a tiny crab grinning as it poked its head out of its shell. George scowled and called out, "Computer! These aren't our T-shirts. The laundry has messed up again."

The female voice responded, "Sorry. I will communicate error to laundry system. Have a nice day!"

"Great," George muttered sarcastically. He glared at the T-shirt and put it on. Calvin, George's younger brother, pulled on the other T-shirt. It read: "Biodiversity Rocks!" It was three sizes too big. Grumpily, they both finished getting dressed.

As they moved towards their bedroom door, something strange happened. The room seemed to tilt. Slightly off balance, Calvin grabbed George's arm. "Whoa! It's another seaquake!"

Then, as suddenly as it began, it ended. Calvin checked on Rex, their goldfish. Unconcerned, Rex swam lazily around in his fishbowl.

A male voice now came over the speakers. "This is Captain Barnaby. The Centre has just experienced a minor seaquake. If you have any concerns, please contact one of the officers."

The boys walked into the kitchen. Their parents were already eating breakfast.

"You're running late," said Dad. "Grab something to eat."

"Did you feel the shake?" George asked.

His mother nodded and frowned. "Yes. That's two this week."

They finished breakfast and got ready to leave. Calvin pushed the button to exit their flat. The door slid back, revealing a long hallway. They waved to neighbours who were also exiting their rooms for the day.

Chapter 2 - Life in a fishbowl

The Centre was a giant dome made of glass and metal. Inside were three levels. The bottom level was where everyone lived. The middle level was the hive of the Centre with research rooms, community areas and the school. The top level was for operations and systems. Only the Captain and officers had access to this level.

The Centre's nickname was WORC, which stood for **W**orld **O**ceanic **R**esearch **C**entre. It was located three thousand metres below the ocean's surface. The purpose of the Centre was to study the ocean deep.

George and Calvin's parents had always dreamed of working at the Centre. Their mother was a marine biologist and their father was a chef. When their application was accepted, they had been thrilled. However, it had taken them time to convince the boys.

"What? We're going to live at the bottom of the sea?" Calvin had exclaimed in horror.

"In a fishbowl, like Rex," George said accusingly.

"Except with air on the inside and water on the outside," Calvin added.

"Come on, now," said Dad. "Where's your sense of adventure? This is a real privilege. Mum and I were chosen from thousands of applicants. It is amazing that we were selected from so many."

"Yes," George agreed, "amazing there were thousands of people crazy enough to want to do it."

Mum laughed. "George, this is the opportunity of a lifetime. For a whole year, we will see areas deep in the ocean that have never been seen before." She ruffled his hair. "Didn't you say you wanted a grand adventure for your tenth birthday?"

"I was talking about a space trip!" George spluttered. (His friend Mina had just returned from a trip to Mars.)

"Well," Dad offered, "think of this as a different type of space."

George made a note to himself: **Be specific when asking for an adventure.**

That was six months ago. George and Calvin had stopped complaining soon after they arrived. The Centre, they decided, was the coolest underwater world ever.

It was located in one of the deepest parts of the ocean. No sunlight came down this far. Their first day onboard, George and Calvin had pressed their faces to the glass walls of the Centre and stared out at a world that seemed totally black. But after a month they began to distinguish flashing lights and creatures outside. They learned that animals that live this deep have interesting features to help them see. Many fish had lights that flashed or glowed. George's favourite was a vivid red deep-sea jellyfish with long trailing webs. Calvin's favourite was a fish called Fangtooth. Its teeth were so large it could not close its mouth.

Chapter 3 - Code red!

The family stepped up to a ramp and waited as it glided upwards. At level two, Mum and Dad went off to work and the boys walked off in the opposite direction. Normally, they would be heading to school but this morning they had training in the Pod Bay. For two weeks, Officer Mei Ling had been teaching them how to operate an underwater ocean pod. These pods were used for deep-water research.

CULCHETH HIGH SCHOOL INDEPENDENT LEARNING CENTRE

"I can't wait to ride in the pod," Calvin raved. "I hope we get to go down near the volcanoes."

"We won't be going anywhere if we don't study for the pod test," George warned him.

Calvin shrugged. "We have lots of time to study for that."

The Pod Bay reminded George of a well-lit cave. In the centre was a large hole filled with ocean water. Two round glass pods bobbed up and down in the water - like giant bubbles.

Officer Mei Ling and two other children were waiting. Gabriela was eleven years old. Bright and patient, she often helped all of them with homework. Berko was nine. A whizz at maths, he was very serious and had a funny habit of stating the obvious.

Gabriela turned to greet them. "Nice shirts," she teased.

Berko asked, "Are you a fan of all isopods? Or just hermit crabs?" George refused to answer. He made a note to himself: **Must find owner of shirt and return it.**

15

Mei Ling called their attention and began the lesson. "Now, if you were taking one of the pods out …" Her sentence was never completed.

A fierce jolt shook the room. It was very different from the one they had felt in the morning. Objects fell off shelves. Equipment tipped over and crashed to the ground. Then the floor seemed to move in a long rolling motion. Cries echoed around the room as they all lost their balance.

George fell onto the floor. Looking up, he saw the pods rocking back and forth. The water underneath the pods was swirling around.

"Get out!" Mei Ling grabbed Calvin and Berko and headed for the door. Gabriela and George followed. But as they neared the door, a red light flashed overhead. "Code red emergency," the computer's voice said. "Pod Bay door has been sealed against flood."

"No!" Mei Ling grabbed the door and tried to pull it open. It would not budge. She slammed her hand against the control panel. "Open the door!" There was no answer.

Chapter 4 - Escape to the pod

Mei Ling pointed out to the water. "We need to get into one of the pods. If the water rises, it could fill the room."

They rushed to the edge of the platform. Getting into one of the pods would be tricky. Along the side of each pod was a short ladder. The ladder led to a door at the top of the pod. The churning water would make it difficult to grab on to the ladder and keep hold of it.

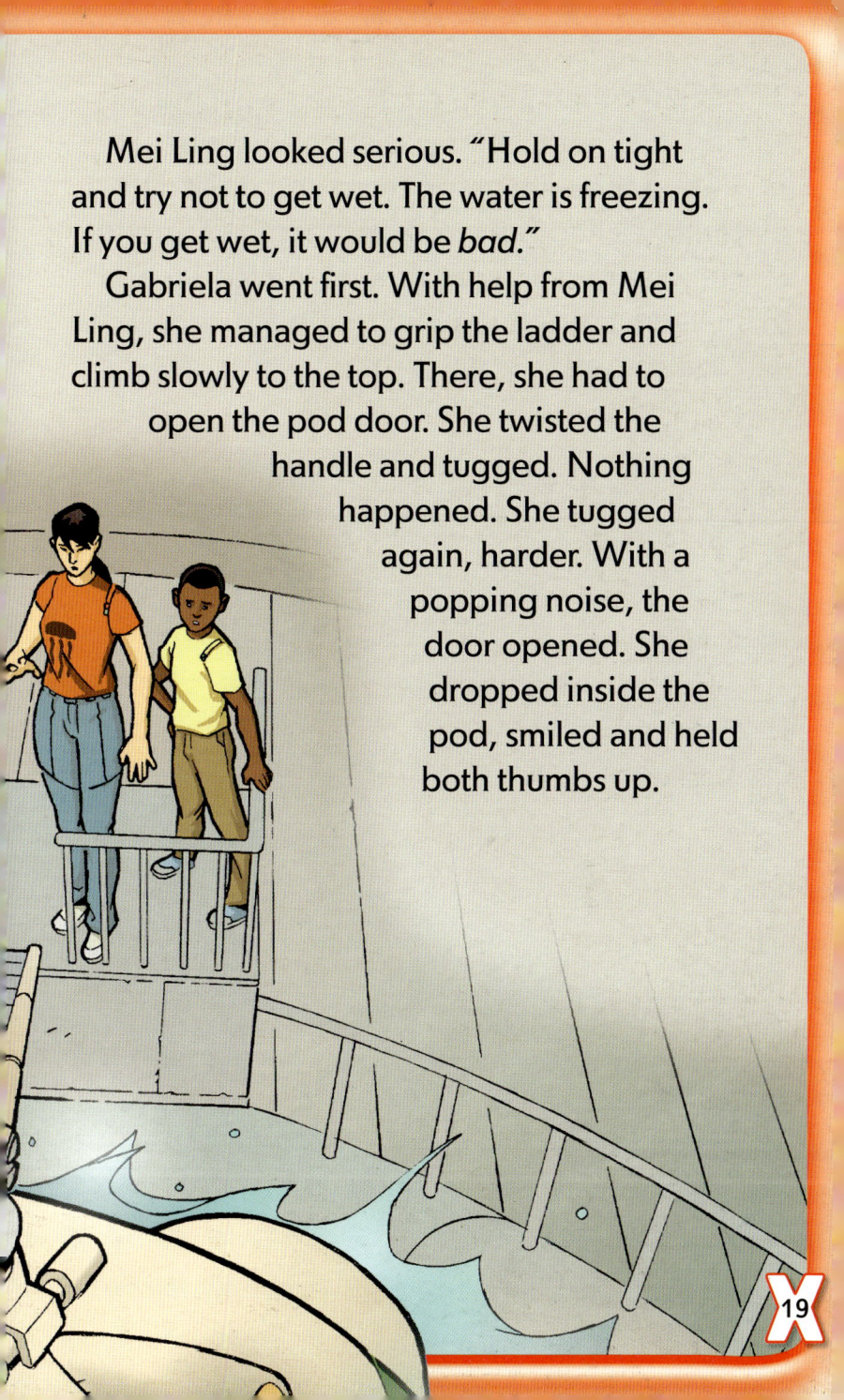

Mei Ling looked serious. "Hold on tight and try not to get wet. The water is freezing. If you get wet, it would be *bad*."

Gabriela went first. With help from Mei Ling, she managed to grip the ladder and climb slowly to the top. There, she had to open the pod door. She twisted the handle and tugged. Nothing happened. She tugged again, harder. With a popping noise, the door opened. She dropped inside the pod, smiled and held both thumbs up.

Calvin then Berko made their way into the pod. George's heart was pounding when it was his turn. He grabbed on and started to climb. As another wave hit the pod, it tipped. He wrapped his arms around the ladder and pulled his legs up as Mei Ling bellowed, "Watch out!"

From inside the pod, the others watched in horror as the pod pushed him towards the water. Then, just as he thought he would become George the Icicle, the pod tipped in the other direction. Quickly, he pulled himself up and climbed into the pod. He was trembling. George made a note to himself: **Avoid situations that involve freezing to death.**

Mei Ling came in last and sealed the door. Through the glass, they could see the water beginning to cover the floor.

Mei Ling announced, "The seaquake is causing the ocean water to flood the room. Once that happens, the water will slam the pod against the walls. So we have to get out of here. Let's see what you've learned." Her voice was grim.

Berko and Calvin took seats next to each other. They would watch the scanners. Gabriela sat at the navigation screen. George sat up front with Mei Ling.

Their seats folded around them, locking them in place. None of the children had ever been in a real pod before. They had only ever had lessons in the simulator. George's gaze fixed on the icy black water. He shivered.

Mei Ling pressed the communication button. "This is Pod One. Can anyone hear me?"

There was silence, then, "This is Captain Barnaby. What is your status?"

Mei Ling told the Captain what had happened. "Try to make your way to the southern Pod Bay," he said. "That area is undamaged. Be careful. The seaquake means the water conditions will be very rough. I'll get you some help."

The pod gave a lurch as another wave hit it. A female voice came over the speaker. "I am ready to assist you to your destination."

"Oh, no!" George groaned. "That's our help? That computer can't even get our laundry right."

The computer was offended. "That was an error by the laundry system, not the central system." George rolled his eyes. Calvin giggled.

"We'll take whatever help we can get," Mei Ling said. She punched in a code. The pod began to hum.

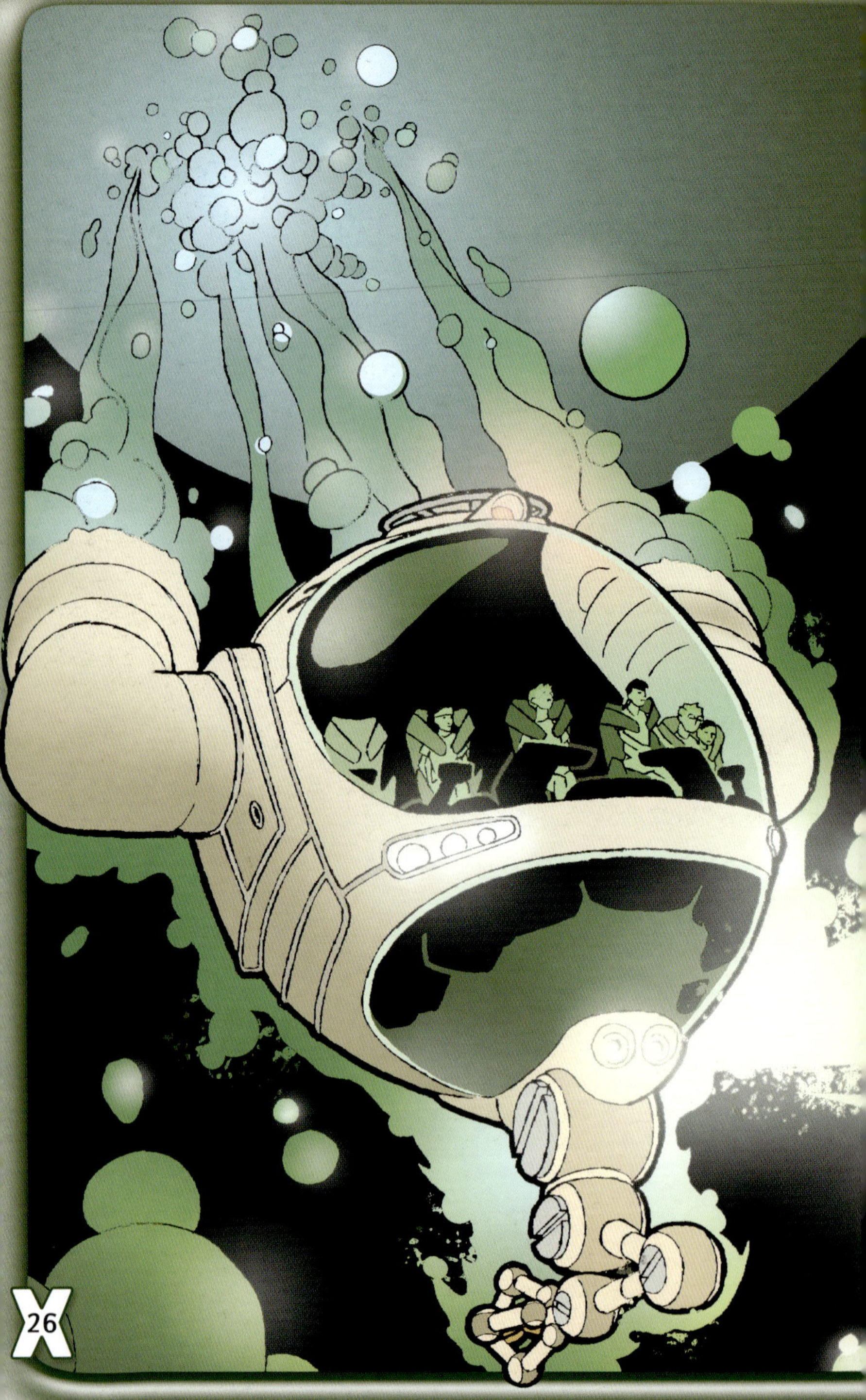

Chapter 5 - Into the darkness

Slowly, the pod sank into the water. Wide eyed, the children watched as the water rose around them. It was like sinking into a pool of ink. "It's really dark," Berko whispered. Then the pod lights came on. Beams of light pierced the darkness in all directions.

Once they had sunk several metres, they saw a large opening that led out into the ocean. Mei Ling called, "Calvin and Berko, watch the scanners. The seaquake will have caused things to move around. Gabriela, talk to the computer. Find the best way to the southern Pod Bay."

Mei Ling considered George. "Can you help me guide her out?" He nodded anxiously. George made a note to himself: **Study for tests in case you are forced to flee in an underwater pod.**

In front of him was the control panel with a bright red line. Following Mei Ling's directions, he raised his right hand and placed a single finger on the centre of the line. Cautiously, he slid his finger forward. The pod moved towards the ocean door. Mei Ling worked the other controls.

"Keep to the centre of the opening," she instructed. George moved his finger to the right. The pod lurched to the right. "Careful," she reminded him. "Use slow, easy movements along the line. It's very sensitive. A little to the left now." Sweating, George slowly moved his finger to the left.

"Great! Just keep it like ... " Again, her sentence was cut off. As they passed through the ocean door, a strong current snatched the pod up. "Hold on!" Mei Ling yelled. The pod spun wildly out of control. Debris and sand flew around them.

George stared out at the stream of cloudy water swirling past. He knew the ocean floor was covered by wide stretches of empty plains. But there were also rocks, mountains and, of course, volcanoes. At any moment they could slam into something. He felt sick.

The pod shuddered as Mei Ling tried to steer them out of the current. The key was not to fight it. They had to slip out sideways. Suddenly, with a jarring pop, they were out. The pod slowed down and came to a stop.

Chapter 6 - Shark!

"Yeah!" The children pumped their fists in the air. The pod now floated quietly above the sandy ocean floor. The lights from the pod illuminated hundreds of sea cucumbers moving along the sand. Jellyfish and shrimp drifted past in a flash of colour. It was a strangely peaceful sight after their wild ride.

Gabriela asked, "Where are we?"

The computer replied, "Location unknown. Navigation sensor has been damaged."

"We're lost," Berko commented.

In order to fix the sensor, Mei Ling would need to go outside. She zipped herself into a thermal ocean suit. It covered her from head to toe. Then she climbed into a room in the back of the pod. After she sealed the door shut, she opened another door that led out to the dark, cold watery world.

Filled with nervous tension, the children watched as Mei Ling swam up to the side of the pod. Repairing the sensor seemed to take forever. They gave loud sighs of relief when she signalled she was done.

Suddenly Gabriela, who had been watching the scanners, gasped. She pointed at the scanner screen. Something was moving towards them. Calvin peered outside to see if he could spot it. "Aaargh!" he cried.

33

A monstrous six-gilled shark emerged from the gloom. First the massive head, then the long powerful body, followed by the swish of its tail. Only found in the deep seas, this shark had six rows of razor-sharp teeth. The shark was probably very hungry. It was hard to find food so far down.

Gabriela screamed as the shark swam nearer. Berko wailed, "This is *bad*!"

Calvin waved frantically to Mei Ling who was still outside the pod. They all joined him, waving and calling out. Mei Ling could not hear them – but she saw them. She looked behind and saw the shark speeding towards her. Now all the children screamed.

"We have to do something," Gabriela said urgently. Mei Ling was pressed against the side of the pod, trying to move slowly towards the back door. The shark was circling.

Chapter 7 - The claw

Calvin grabbed George's arm. "The claw!"

George slapped his forehead. "Of course, the claw." He ran to one of the control panels and feverishly searched through the menu choices. He pressed his finger against the option marked *claw*. A whirring noise filled the pod.

Calvin, Gabriela and Berko screamed. The shark had lunged at Mei Ling. She was still one metre from the door. The shark knocked her into the pod. There was a dull thud as her head hit the glass.

"Hurry!" Calvin screeched.

The claw was a large metal hand, used to grab things outside of the pod. As the claw swung out from under the pod, George tried to aim it at the shark. It missed, but the motion distracted the beast. It backed off.

Calvin was scared. "Mei Ling isn't moving. We need to get her into the pod." Berko nodded.

Gabriela bit her lip. Then she suggested, "We could use the claw to get her inside."

George made a decision. "OK. I'll try to move the pod between Mei Ling and the shark."

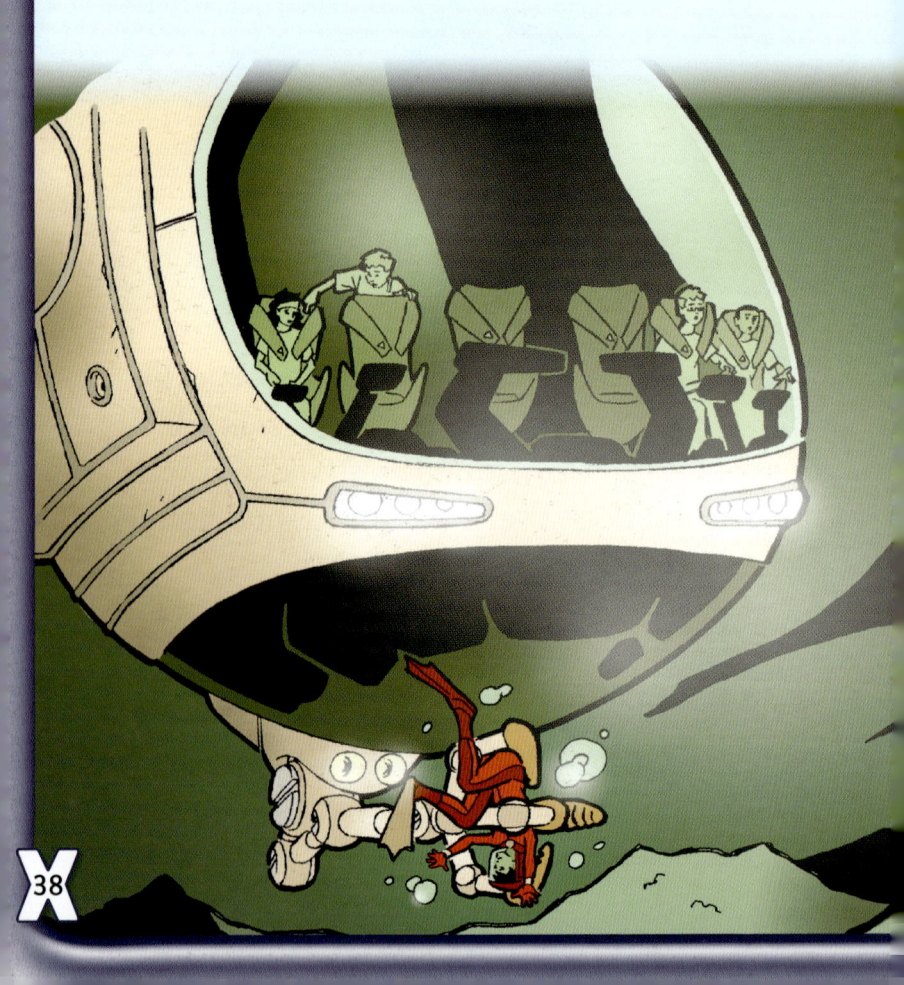

Gabriela began working the controls for the claw. George ran to the front of the pod. Carefully, he moved his finger along the red line. The pod shifted. Mei Ling had floated to the left of the pod. The shark was a few metres away. As quickly as he could, George moved the pod in front of the shark. The claw whirred as Gabriela tried to hook Mei Ling.

The shark, separated from its prey, slammed into the pod. George gave a loud yell. He found himself facing a huge gaping mouth stuffed with generous pointed teeth. George made a note to himself: **Avoid putting yourself in front of a mad shark.**

"Do you have her?" George called out anxiously.

"Almost." Gabriela sounded equally tense.

"Hurry. This shark isn't looking happy." George gave a nervous shudder. "And it has abnormally large teeth!"

"Got her!" Gabriela yelled.

George called to the computer. "Open the back door and get her inside." Berko, Gabriela and Calvin ran to the back room. George stayed up front with the shark.

Chapter 8 - Scary shortcut

The back room was warm. Mei Ling was lying on the floor. The children pulled the hood off her head. Her eyes were closed, but she was breathing. "She's unconscious," Berko observed.

"Is she OK?" Calvin asked quietly.

Gabriela put a medical sensor on Mei Ling's forehead. "That should help her," she whispered.

George called to them and they ran out front. Silently, he pointed. The shark had company. Swimming lazily next to the pod was an enormous gulper eel. Its long tail swayed threateningly as it swam past. The gulper eel has a giant mouth that can swallow prey as big as itself. The children gasped as a third fish arrived. It was very large and mean-looking. It came at them, spiked teeth jutting from its mouth. "Fangtooth!" Calvin exclaimed.

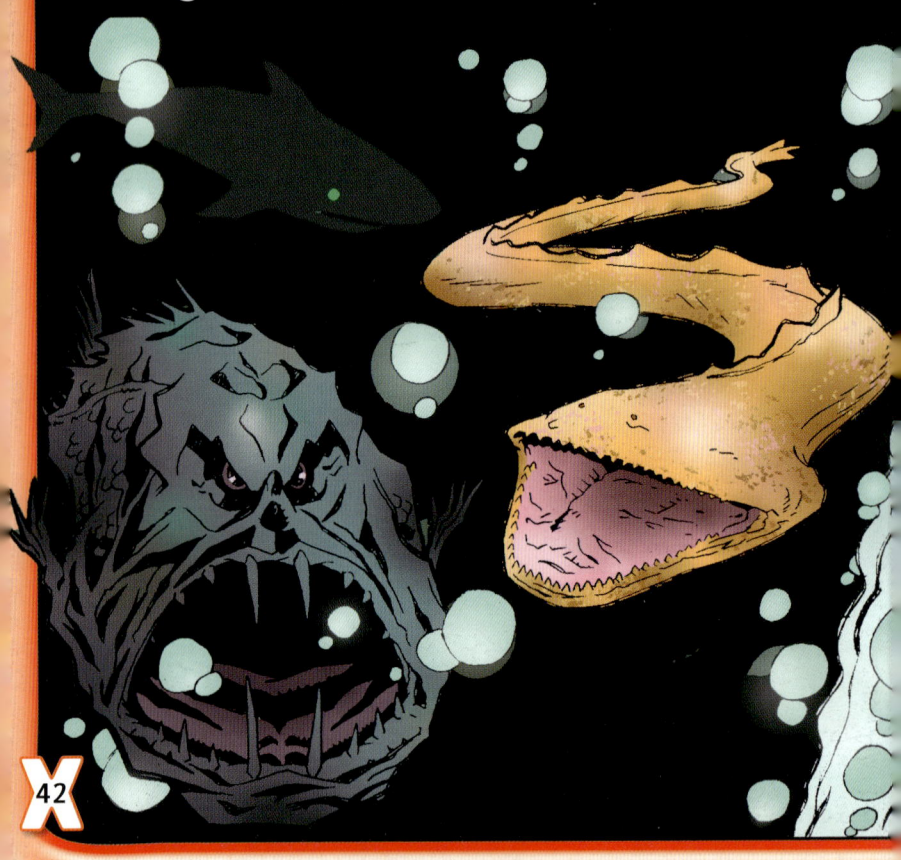

"We should move," Berko said.

George and Gabriela took the seats at the front. Berko and Calvin sat next to the scanners. Gabriela read the navigation screen. "There are two ways back to the Centre. The shortcut takes us past the volcanoes. Or we can go through the plains. It will take longer but it is easier."

The computer spoke: "The pod will run out of oxygen in 13 minutes, 41 seconds."

They all looked at each other. "Well then, I guess it's the volcanoes," George said dryly. "That should make Calvin happy." Gabriela yelped as the gulper eel brushed against the pod.

The path through the volcanoes would be dangerous. Towering mountains and harsh jagged rocks filled the landscape. Heavy steam from the volcanoes was hot enough to melt the pod – and everything inside it.

George had once dreamed of taking out an underwater pod. Of course, in the dream he had known what he was doing. He also recalled he had not been terrified. George made a note to himself: **Next time stick to the dream.**

Chapter 9 - Deadly steam bath

"Turn east and proceed for two miles," the computer said. George moved his finger along the red line.

They passed massive mountains of lava and ash. Searing clouds of sulphur gushed from the sides and tops of the volcanoes. Light from the pod fell on different parts of the rock walls. Shrimp and mussels clung bravely to the sides of huge pillars of solid lava. It was an eerie underwater scene.

Suddenly, an enormous fountain of steam shot from the volcano on their right. The children screamed. In a panic, George jerked his finger to the left but too quickly. The pod swung wildly, heading straight towards a large and solid mass of rocks. More screaming. George corrected the movement – and then they were clear.

Berko whispered, "That was really scary."

Gabriela croaked, "My throat hurts from screaming so much."

Calvin enthused, "Volcanoes are so cool!"

Frozen from fear, George merely grunted. He made a note to himself: **Avoid situations that involve certain death.**

They continued their journey through the chain of volcanoes. Berko studied the map. Gabriela peered ahead anxiously. The computer, blissfully unconcerned, directed them forward.

"The largest volcano is up ahead," Calvin informed them.

They gaped. Rising hundreds of metres overhead, it loomed over them. Across from the volcano was a sheer rock wall that went up and up. The pod would need to travel between these two gigantic structures. A furious burst of steam made them all jump.

"Oh, boy," George muttered.

"Turn south in 850 metres," the computer said.

"In less than a kilometre, we'll be liquefied," George grumbled.

Berko offered, "We could try getting around the steam." There was a long silence.

"Right," George said. "Any other suggestions?" There was another long silence. "OK, all in favour of a deadly steam bath, raise their hands." All hands went up.

George nodded glumly, "Steam bath it is."

49

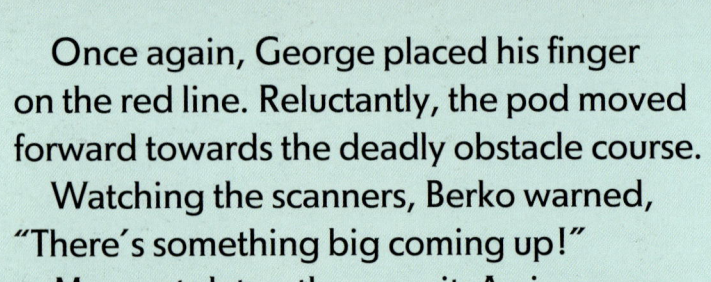

Once again, George placed his finger on the red line. Reluctantly, the pod moved forward towards the deadly obstacle course.

Watching the scanners, Berko warned, "There's something big coming up!"

Moments later, they saw it. An immense boulder had fallen and partially blocked their path.

George tried to steer the pod over it, but up ahead a gush of steam spiralled through the water.

"Get above the steam!" Gabriela yelled. George moved them further up. Another jet of steam burst out from another vent overhead. Startled, George's hand jerked and the pod shot towards the steam. They all screamed. "No!"

Gabriela pointed wildly at the floor. "Down!"

The pod shot downwards towards the rocky ground. They continued to scream as George weaved them crazily through the last few metres. Then, with a suddenness that caused them to gasp, not scream, they were clear. They were out from between the mountains. They stared. All around them were vast plains of sand. And, directly in front of them, was the Centre.

Chapter 10 - Home at last!

"We did it!" they cheered. The computer directed them to the southern Pod Bay. Luckily, Gabriela remembered how to bring the pod up to the surface. She turned off the engine. All was quiet.

"Well," George grunted, his throat dry from terror. "That wasn't so bad."

"Yes," Gabriela replied, her hands still shaking. "Let's all do that again sometime."

"We're definitely not dead," Berko commented as he pinched himself.

"And we got to see the volcanoes!" Calvin said excitedly.

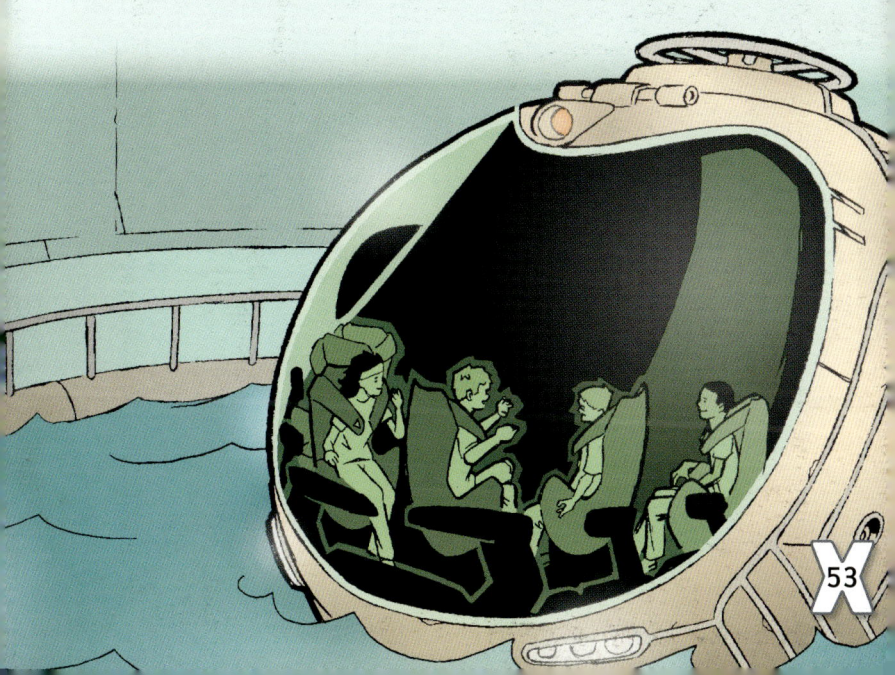

Then they saw people hurrying towards their pod. George and Calvin could see their parents waving.

Mei Ling stumbled out from the back. "What happened?" She looked outside and gasped. "You got us back by yourselves?" They laughed and hugged her. "Wow! I must be a better teacher than I thought," she said.

Captain Barnaby was waiting to help each of them out. As George climbed down, the Captain grinned and eyed his shirt. "I see the laundry system sent you one of my T-shirts."

George looked down. "Do you mind if I keep it? This shirt and I have been through a lot."

Captain Barnaby smiled. "Happy to see it find a good home." He leaned forward and whispered, "My mother sends them to me and I'm always trying to 'lose' them." He pointed to his shirt. It read: "Fish are my best friends". It had a picture of a smiling shark on it. It was truly the worst T-shirt George had ever seen. He made a note to himself: **Thank laundry system for not giving me that shirt!**

AMAZING DEEP SEA FACTS

- Oceans cover over 70% of the Earth's surface.
- The deep sea is the largest habitat for living things on our planet.
- The deepest part of the ocean is 11 kilometres
- The largest waterfall on earth (the Denmark Strait Cataract) lies underwater.
- The temperature of most of the deep sea is only just above freezing.
- More people have travelled into space than have travelled to the deepest parts of the ocean.
- The gulper eel unhinges its jaws and stretches its stomach to swallow fish bigger than itself.
- Most of the world's volcanoes are found underwater.

Can you find some other amazing deep sea facts?